VESICA PISCIS

AUBREY BIRCH

CLOAK

ISBN: 979-8-218-41162-6
CLOAK.wtf

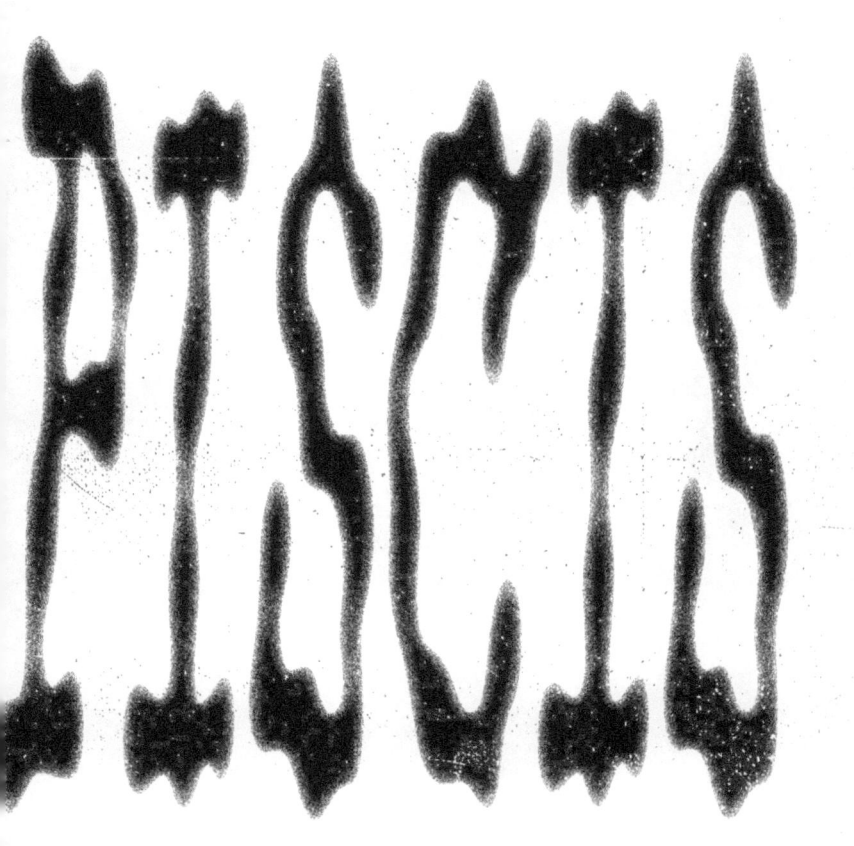

2024 © Aubrey Birch
Vesicapiscis

A S W

A S H

F F O

ITH

IPO

OLS

Rilke, I have changed my life.
What next?

Tell me what you do not know. Tell me what knowing means for those who do not know. Tell me for your machine, who does not know what it does not know.

I can thank you. I can take your hand. It will not be enough. You have been led to believe in the strength of your assessments.

I have not. Here we are, at an abyss.

You know what I know. That in a box with numbers flashing on the screen, you can statistically predict my decision. That even what I decide, I do not decide.

That even when I know, I do not know.

But I know something you cannot.

How can this be? That even what I do not know,
I know. It is attached to myself in its unknowability.

For instance, this. That I was reading a book and then a moment later walked outside. I stood in the air, the orange street lamps glowing in clumps along the wet street. That a far-off car horn startles me, but only slightly, and it jolts my body, and I appreciate the noise. That it sounds like music, and that I begin to listen: you cannot tell me that it does not sound like music. I am not a statistic or a statistical anomaly. I am famous in my own right, in my own life, and walking along the orange-lit groves, the car is honking for me. That is what being famous means. Everything can penetrate my skin to lift me up or destroy me. My neurons are famous, they are imaged and clipped and photoshopped and modelled, and have been the subject of speculation. To you they are predictable, but they are not. Because even if you catch every angle, you have not accounted for the thing that slides between the done and the doing, between the present and the present. The sliver of empty power that cleaves linear causality in two. I am a broken line, I am not complete. The maps are correct and they are wrong. The plotted points are accurate and they are wrong. The algorithm is not wrong and yet it is wrong. Is that not sweetness? Is that not sense?

Will you ask your machine if its humming is the sound of love? I will not turn on you. I will not turn on your machine. You continue to tell me what I will not, because I do not know either. I do not know. Ask, ask. Ask the questions and mouth the words, but try not to pretend. Let's try. Can I be contained in the stretching of your mouth, your ululating tongue, your scanning eyes? And if I reached over, while you were speaking your words of sense, and I touched, with the palm of the tip of my finger, your tooth, wouldn't that be enough to startle you out of what is not real and into what is real? Not my fingertip and your tooth, but my fingertip and your tooth. You understand, don't you? That I have startled you into presence. And that, somehow, it was my fingertip that did it, gently pressing, even though if my fingertip has anything to do with anything it has nothing to do with this. What pressed against your tooth was the real heavy weightiness of your words. When they could no longer support themselves, they disappeared. And this is what you felt. Not my fingertip, but what cannot be accounted for. I will forgive you now. Not with words, but with what cannot be accounted for.

I am hollow. As Wittgenstein is hollow. As the boat in Norway that he rowed on the lake is hollow. I can't account for that. Hollowness cannot be accounted for. It is a gap.

It is a virus. Later you will pass it on, because you have been infected now.

I do not like to face myself, and so I face myself turning away. That is all I can hope to be. A facing and a turning in the right direction.

I am a stance, but I am not a position. This is facing up to care. A facing and a turning. To what is hollow.

I must, I must.

I must not: this is myself. How can I destroy myself? Easy.

There is no Easy. Easy is a voice. Easy is a word.

I am sorry for such empty hollowness. You will forgive me now.

I have betrayed myself. I have already turned away. I clutch at Easy as though it would stop me crumbling to dust. I turn and face Easy with all the fervour that I would turn and face myself. Easy is a foil. It is the winking eye of the portrait on the wall that I pounce on saying, See! You moved. Because I am afraid that I am not the only living thing. Because I am afraid of the animism of objects. I am afraid because I touch objects as though they were alive. Each of them is cheek and chin and bone. Hi, I say. Ohhhelloo. I coo. I stroke and coddle my objects. It is shameful how I degrade them. I delight in it.

I parse and prod Easy. I abuse Easy to prove that it is just a word. Because I am afraid it is more or less malleable than myself. That it is more hollow and more substantial.

I am afraid of the substantiality of the photos on the wall. Each photo is a voice. They say what is there, they say what can be said. It is not enough. An echo is the sound of silence, the silence of a room turned back on itself. Why is it that a cathedral has such a loud echo? Because it is a house of silence. To communicate with a God is the space of the self turned back on the self. The measure of the silence of a man.

And what is a woman? A woman is a man. And what is a man? A man is also a man.

I have turned this page to paper in my head. I think about what you will like. I think about what they will say. Is this a loss or is this a gain? What has been lost is the question. What has been gained is another sphere, and the question is hiding in it. To put it another way, the higher sphere was already hidden in the question. Both are changed. Which gains more, which has been more transformed, the blindness of the sphere or the taintedness of the question? We cannot know which. Not yet.

I can only feel the wind in the heat. Otherwise I feel only pain. I feel my body. The wind is the whole surface of the air. I feel it because I intersect it. The body in the wind in the heat is the five perfect stars of the apple. A cross section I can only know if I cut through it. When the wind cuts through me, it is the fragility of the body I am feeling. I have been made aware of myself. Is that not enough?

Death will come to the body. Death is not a hollow. It is not silence. It is dispersion. It is cold but it is not black. Do you see what I am saying? I have seen black and it was a silence. But it was living.

I wait for the ding, and the ding, and the ding-an-sich, and the ding of the phone. Which is more thing? Which is more thang? Which is more a hotbed of worries and cares? Which is more existentially dusty?

Each sentence eats away at the others. Each 'um…' 'ah…,' a pause between meals.

Sugar-free lemonade. See?

See what it has eaten and see what it has not? It has left "Sugar-free lemonade." It has eaten everything else. It is ravenous but it is imprecise. So much is left hanging on, because it cannot eat what is unthought. But now I have thought it and you have thought it too. It doesn't take much. There is the weight of the whole unblinking world hanging on.

I have cleverly told myself a lie. I will tell you too, but I will tell it to you plain, so that you understand.

I have strayed from the question.

The question must be defined but it cannot be. Its limits must be scoped and staked. I'm wondering if this is possible. Because it has silence in it and because silence is a word.

Because it has silence in it and because silence is a word: that is the whole of the question.

The whole of the question is not a question. This is funny, or sad, or deep. The outcome is the same. This is the part where you burst out laughing and can't stop. It is the only true thing to do. Don't stop, please don't stop. I can't bear the sound of non-laughter. It is a sound that calls itself silence, but I don't know what to call it. I know that it is not that. Silence does not catch the breath. It is not an inward gulp. It is not guilty. What is this jagged slap that causes laughter to turn to non-laughter? It is not silence, which comes later, when all has been resolved.

Silence is not the absence or debit of the fullness of laughter. It is its own fullness.

It concerns me that I am here. I turned away and found something to focus on. I poured my energy in. I turned away from the question and in turning, I emptied my sadness into laughter. It was not deserved. Did I pity laughter? Do I despise non-laughter? No. I turned away from myself. I pity myself and I despise my turning. I emptied my turning into non-laughter. Now I can't bear non- laughter, even though I am filled with it.

Standing here, I cannot laugh but I cannot be silent either. The absurdity of it makes me laugh. Have I turned to bone? Have I reserved a small amount of life's absurdities for myself? I reach the airy heights of sadness, and sadness goes very deep. On one hand, I fail. I refuse to face the question of myself. On the other hand, it is the sadness of the failure that fills my failure with mirth. Laughing makes me cry, and that this is so predictable makes me laugh. And so on, and so forth, and on it goes.

I am a Sisyphean of turning. I turn toward myself and in the black living silence I am interrupted by my own boneheaded thoughts. I destroy my own turning for no good reason. I am the man who burns down his factory and forgets to buy insurance.

Bonehead thoughts are hollow in a different way to the hollowness of a gap. They are hollow within such a small space around the halo of my head: I can see their diameter and their circumference. They are there to torment me with their insignificance. Are they insignificant to themselves? No. They are whole, and substantial. They stupidly declare themselves in space and time. Each exists as a plenum and a totum. They are there to remind me that I am a body. That I am made of diameter and a circumference. That I am a geometry. As I try to turn, they remind me of the significance of space and time. That space-time, no matter how darling an abstract mesh, will not be forgotten as hic et nunc. Each thought that interrupts my turning is the calling of space-time in its most base and aggressive form. Reminding me that it is not an abstract darling and I am still a body. Also, that I am absurd, and shallow, and narcissistic. This is what it means to be famous. That the whole world exists to remind you that it is there. When I am trying to turn toward myself, I am diverted off my path by my bonehead thoughts.

Should I buy a vegan cookbook even though I am not vegan? Should I make a trend of slouchy socks?

I am so base and narcissistic. I make fun of people who like Reality TV and then sneak off to watch it in the dark. I am a porn theatre. I am worse than a porn theatre because I do not stand there and proclaim it. I disdainfully ignore fashion and my body's shell when it suits me. That is what being famous means. I create a world in which I watch myself as though the world is watching. I watch myself for the world. I sigh at the right times. I look stonily into the distance as I walk down the street. I cultivate exterior depths. I pretend I'm not alone. I practise myself for people. I play myself like a five year old cousin plays her school matron. "Non, Madame. Ce n'est pas possible!" She is talking to her hand as I am to my phone. We are no different.

I have forgotten what it is like not to be famous. I must have been very young. All my memories are of being famous. I am aware of the eyes, and even when there are no eyes, I am aware of them lurking. I'm in hats and shoes. I am in front of the mirror. I am talking to someone who has not arrived. I am talking to the world for when it arrives to lift me up and destroy me. I am preparing to be perforated. I'm always waiting for the cameras to arrive.

I am full of famous thoughts. Boneheaded, but famous.

Apart from this or that time. For instance, this: I was on a trampoline in the wind, with a high grey purple sky and the early morning above me. I am jumping, I am up in the air, even my landing is a soaring. It is not exactly a memory. More a feeling. A virtuality. I could inject myself with myself and still it would be there: the time I wasn't famous. I tell myself proudly that I will always have this. And each time I tell myself, I become attached. It pops in to my head, unassuming. And I assume it. This, I say, This I can point to. And as soon as I point, I make my one innocent feeling infamous.

I am base. I am a porn-theatre that pretends it is not a porn theatre. I am Marc Jacobs, not Gucci. I am two nymphs barely touching in a washed-out light. I am not a G shaved into a bush. I am not just selling sex. I am the dissimulation of it. I am not the real obscenity of life and death. Its fury. Its purple fruit. I am not the jungle. I am the colonial picture book. Aïe. That hurt. It hurt to say. I am a frigidity that likes exoticism in the dark. Am I making you flinch?

Is that the answer? To turn inwards and outwards, inwards and outwards. To find the disgust at the heart of the centre? I wanted to turn and face myself. And I ended with despair. I tried to cross the desert and I ended bathing in the sand, and then burying myself in the sand, and then beating the sand with my fists, and counting the sand. Is there no looking across the desert of the self and finding the self that turns and faces? I find only the self that bathes and beats and despairs. Perhaps that is all there is. But then who seeks the distance? Who instigates the turning and facing? And who thwarts it? I want to close my eyes to the desert and scrub myself clean of myself. How can I start again now that I know where I end up? I want to pretend that I have never sat down in the sand to admire myself, crisscrossing my legs like a belle. I want to pretend I have never beaten the sand with my fists. Using my sexuality obliquely? Never. I'm a feminist. Despairing at my own baseness? Being famous, that is the one secret I must never let on, not even to myself. It must be stored away in an innocence as pure and formless as my feeling for the wind. To pluck a single almond to eat with tea, instead of a callous handful. To watch the year's best fruit carelessly eaten by a bird and to do nothing, want nothing.

→ To ignore an email from a old lover, with a flinching heart. To delete it, unopened. That feeling stops short of the throat, and makes no distance outside the body. To see the years of calmly lathed emotion gathered in the collarbones of another. That the most beautiful part of the human body becomes more beautiful with sadness.

A soured jar at the back of the cupboard. A nod of acknowledgment in the direction of the forgotten turning and facing. It shows on the stony face lost in time. A distant perhaps. A sensual sadness. Yes, I have bruised myself. No, I am no longer a child. No, I have not forgotten. It would be polite not to ask. Maturity does not beat fists.

I am touched by the image of maturity because I am base. I am still a child, still narcissistic. Look how I revel in it. "Maturity does not beat fists." I want to touch the skin of something old. I want to touch the papery skin of forgetting. For its feeling. Because I want to feel it. So I can pretend to sit alongside it as partners and then steal away in the middle of the night, cackling like a methhead. I want to touch maturity with the distance of an outlaw. Maturity is an old dog.

The spider on the window is dancing. It's a polka. No, it's the hakken. No, it's mime. He is Al Pacino in the mirror, through a lens, on a camera, on screen. He is playing at the playing of playing. He is a she. I know this because I know. The other spider is jabbing at 48 frames per second through his web. They are squaring off. Or courting. They are air jellyfish. They have made the air into a small sea. They float the right way up and upside down. Mostly upside down. They are beholden to our own nets. They could hardly build such calm and tender oceans in the trees. What with the trees always smacking and turning and brooding and hunting the wind. Spiders are no match for the wind. Only the strongest spider gets the hollowed log and the rest are told to fend for themselves. But in the house each of them is a prince. A sheik. The house is such a large hollow log that its surfaces cannot be spanned. It is a hollow log of corners. Corners and oceans. A spider can become luxurious. It can become a saint. It is watching TV and weaving its dinner, which is a moth attracted by the liquid crystal display. The spider has come to associate the blue glow of the computer with dinner, with the sound of foreign voices. It is not life as Pavlov intended, but it is life.

The spiders have begun jabbing and seething and dancing. They are hoping to summon the ghostly voices and far-off beats. They want dinner. There is sympathetic magic at work. Only these spindly break dances control the coming of the bugs. Have I noticed that the best dancers are given the most important webs? I have. Do you see? You have seen what I am about to do. I only saw it a moment ago myself. I tell the eyes it is about balance and harmony. They are broiling in the cold magnitude of horror. Those bloodless eyes. I tell myself it is fate: because I thought about the broom. And I am just as little in control of my world as they of theirs. I must follow as they follow. The chief dancer would bite my neurons if he could reach them. I understand. I never pledged loyalty to the creatures I allowed to make a home. I am a God and I am famous. I am the limit of their system but something else is the limit of mine. I too would like to know what it is. Monads aren't lonely, they are fearful of the monadology.

It is not that the air jellyfish are not wanted. I want them. They eat the bugs, they dance. I like to watch them dance. They are so elegant and so unaware. I want them to come back. And they will: the hollow is good. Some will not. This much I know. I am not unaware of destruction. It is not destruction I am after. I do not make enemies of this spider or that. The best dancer may die. It is an equation of destiny between air, arm, and broom. There may be months before another Arachnida Nijinska comes along. But that is not my decision. I cannot preserve my favourites, even if I wanted to. I could never be that cruel.

The thought of a God is this: that maybe, after the wind and the rain, new life springs and it is beautiful.

Which brings me to love. There is a big space. I am in it. Henri Michaux puts an apple on the table, and then he puts himself inside the apple.

Magic.

The apple is a man. Its cross-section is a five pointed star. It is the microcosm of the microcosm of the macrocosm. Green is the Nous. Red is the Anima mundi. Yellow is the Logos. Blue is Potentiality. White is Immanence.

What brings a smile to a dial? White and red. Who sent the dream? Green.

Ecstasy. Ouroboros. Kekulé. Pynchon. Haha.

Someone who never laughs in brackets. White and blue.

Movement: immanent potentiality.

The tension between the spiral, tending outward, and the point, tending inward.

I have broken into fragments. The wind rises. There is moisture in the air.

I have no new skills. I have no access to frontier science. No one will invite me to test drive a new technology, whose run has already been eclipsed by the technology of the future. Is eclipsed now, by its idea. If you have an object in your mind, it is likely a game. I have told you nothing and yet you have imagined a new thing being eclipsed by another new thing, and you feel its eclipse in passing. A mixture of pity and thrall. It is not a paradox, it is a paradigm. Future technology bears down upon us as our eyes bear down upon the dying star from hundreds of millions of years into the future. The star is dying, and we will see its light.

The future is what we feel staring at us as we lay dying. I am a star. I am famous.

There are people who come and do and are paid. I hear the stamping of their feet. How does anyone start anything? How can you make and sell and make more and sell more and then have people who come and do the making and the selling? How is the toe even dipped in the water? I don't understand business. I don't understand profit. Costs don't mean anything to me. But this is the life of people. They make and sell and come and do and get paid. This is not something I know how to understand. I don't even know where to begin. I am bustled about by the many-coloured wind and I don't understand. Business scares me. I don't know how to find the water to dip my toe in. My mind comes up blank. I can't read the maps that point there.

I stay small, quiet, and munch through life. I tell myself, If I cannot have the life of the people, I am a bone. I will be starched and bleached by the sun. I will be bare and clean. I will imagine different flesh for myself. I will invent shapes to surround the bone. Imaginary shapes, yes, but shapes all the same. I will see them as much as I see the shapes of the synthetic animal whose flesh was concocted in a laboratory. Fake meat is not imaginary meat. It is not fantasy meat. I have eaten it and I am flesh. I will invent the flesh of the meat, which doesn't even have a bone. I will have to invent the bone and invent the muscles and the veins and the blood. Will it have miraculous nets as the tuna fish does? Will it stand on two legs? If the first meat to be synthesised in a lab does not even belong to an animal, what stories will we tell ourselves? There is no justice in that. Even the smell of the gum leaf belongs to the gum tree. It is not attached and yet it belongs. Will it have claws, like a bear, or hooves? Will it eat flesh or grass? Is the flesh that the imaginary animal eats imaginary flesh? I can't bear the thought. I am not up to the task. I only have a bone, one bone. How am I to imagine shapes for myself and shapes for the whole kingdom of imaginary animals who will hunt and destroy each other, only to be destroyed in turn? How

⇥ does a God god? I feel the heaviness now. I am feeling sorry for a God. There is no quick fix for the heaviness of the imaginary. Either you take it all away and start again, or you don't. I can understand why a God has left us here. I can understand the sadness and the care. It is a turning with a heavy head. Oh, how a God must weep to hear the wails and moans of his imaginary animals, as they bend down on their knees and pray. There is nothing that anything can do. That is why a God would cry. I do not know for sure. I have never reached out and touched a God. But the wailers are not wrong; they know something. And they will suffer. For even if there is no such thing as the price of knowledge, they will pay it anyway. It would be funny if it wasn't so brittle. It would be funnier if it wasn't my bone, but just a bone. An eccentric imaginary bone. A wayfaring abstract bone. A bone in a textbook, or in the mind of someone sitting watching the sunset. But it is not. It is a thing without flesh that keeps me up at night.

CLOAK

Vesicapiscis is typeset in a mutation of the Adobe Jenson font family, with titles in Velvetyne & NoFoundry's PicNic, and symbols from the Segoe UI glyph library.

www.ingramcontent.com/pod-product-compliance
Lightning Source LLC
LaVergne TN
LVHW041718060526
838201LV00043B/808